DRAMA TEAM SKETCHBOOK

12 Scripts That Bring the Gospels to Life

ALISON SIEWERT

InterVarsity Press
Downers Grove, Illinois

InterVarsity Press
P.O. Box 1400, Downers Grove, IL 60515-1426
World Wide Web: www.ivpress.com
E-mail: mail@ivpress.com

InterVarsity Press® is the book-publishing division of InterVarsity Christian Fellowship/USA®, a student movement active on campus at hundreds of universities, colleges and schools of nursing in the United States of America, and a member movement of the International Fellowship of Evangelical Students. For information about local and regional activities, write Public Relations Dept., InterVarsity Christian Fellowship/USA, 6400 Schroeder Rd., P.O. Box 7895, Madison, WI 53707-7895, or visit the IVCF website at <www.ivcf.org>.

Scripture quotations, unless otherwise noted, are from the New Revised Standard Version of the Bible, copyright 1989 by the Division of Christian Education of the National Council of the Churches of Christ in the USA. Used by permission. All rights reserved.

Permission is granted to perform the sketches in noncommercial settings as long as one copy of the book is provided to each actor. If a ticket fee is charged, then please contact InterVarsity Press for permission.

Cover design: Cindy Kiple

Images: stool: C Squared Studios/Getty Images
director chair: Ryan McVay/Getty Images
wooden chair: C Squared Studios/Getty Images
ladder: Photodisc Collection/Getty Images
man looking: Henrik Sorenson/Getty Images
man sitting: Lise Metzger/Getty Images

ISBN 0-8308-3208-4

Printed in the United States of America ∞

Library of Congress Cataloging-in-Publication Data

Siewert, Alison.
   Drama team sketchbook: 12 scripts that bring the Gospels to life /
Alison Siewert.
     p. cm.
   ISBN 0-8308-3208-4 (pbk.: alk. paper)
   1. Bible stories, English—N.T. Gospels. 2. Christian drama,
American. I. Title.
   BS551.3.S545 2004
   246'.72—dc22

2003018830

P	22	21	20	19	18	17	16	15	14	13	12	11	10	9	8	7	6	5	4	3	2	1
Y	21	20	19	18	17	16	15	14	13	12	11	10	09	08	07	06	05	04	03			

With thanks to Daniel,

who encouraged, animated and refined

many of these sketches.

If the canoe sinks,

walk on water.

Courage, hope, art.

CONTENTS

INTRODUCTION

When you're in trouble, you need a hero.

That reality has powered storytelling from ancient nomadic campfires to the latest Saturday morning cartoons. And throughout human history, people have told the hero's story not just through words but through words acted out: drama.

Many of us grew up seeing the story on flannelboards with flat, felt figures representing the great people of faith. *Look, kids! This little stick figure is Moses. You can tell because he's got little felt tablets in his hands (well, actually stuck to his little felt robe), while the other felt guy, Aaron, is carrying a yellow felt cow idol. Boo, Aaron! Yay, Moses!*

Once we outgrew the flannel, we went to worship and heard the stories of faith . . . recited by guys in robes reading books with gilt edges, intoning thees and thous. You'd think God is the most formal being ever to have lived. And to be honest, he seems a little, well, dry. Distant. Perhaps even boring.

But the story of Jesus is *the* hero's tale. It's not boring, and it's not flat.

Jesus' story is more scandalous than a novel and more thrilling than the most frenzied action flick. Dorothy Sayers said Jesus

was tender to the unfortunate, pa-tient with honest inquirers, and humble before Heaven; but He in-sulted respectable clergymen by calling them hypocrites. . . . He went to parties in disreputable company. . . . He assaulted indig-nant tradesmen and threw them and their belongings out of the Temple. . . . He drove a coach-and-horses through a number of sacro-sanct and hoary regulations; He cured diseases by any means that came handy, with a shocking casu-alness in the matter of other peo-ple's pigs and property; He showed no proper deference for wealth or social position. . . . He was emphat-ically not a dull man in his life-time, and if He was God, there can be nothing dull about God, either.[1]

It's a great story, and it really ought to be told well. The gospel is supposed to come off as good news, not as a goofy af-terthought or a deadbeat drone on the meaning of life. If this book helps you tell the gospel story like it's a story and as though it's pretty interesting, then great. That's what I'm hoping for.

WHY DRAMA?

Drama is the compression of our expe-rience into a story we can watch on a stage. It's a way of communicating what's valuable, how we got here, what we're hoping for. Drama describes our condition, and creates symbols and stories in which we find release.

We need to think about drama because it is everywhere. Murray Watts says, "Drama, largely because of technological factors, has become the dominant form of artistic communication in the western world."[2] People like drama because it allows them to project, to process, to relate their own lives to the staged lives of characters. Maybe we don't always think of it this way, but television is a dramatic medium. It may be in large part a sick and frivolous one, but it thrives on drama—whether it's good or bad, cheap or deep.

You can figure out a lot even in an unfamiliar culture by watching its dramas. Think about how much of Elizabethan England we know through Shakespeare, or what we know of Greek society through its plays. Aeschylus, Puccini, August Wilson, Zhang Yimou, The Fugees—all have created stories through which we understand human cultures and human hearts.

Drama is a language our world understands, a coin of the realm. Erudite, rational discourse has its place, and so do textual studies. But drama does something for us that a sermon or a theological treatise cannot. It evokes rather than explains. It gives access to experience. Drama taps into what's

deeply felt and intuitive. Dramatic forms hold heightened importance for the church in the postmodern age. They need to carry more weight, not less. And our theatrical work needs to be good—really good.

Slick and powerful—even manipulative—dramatic entertainment is what our culture expects and gives its attention to. We are not called to reproduce that. As Calvin Seerveld observes, "Art, like anything else, is relevant if it supplies what is needed. Art that is popular is supplying what is wanted, but not necessarily what is needed."[3] We have an opportunity to make art with quality and substance—art that reflects what's truly important, whether popular or not.

The world needs to hear the gospel, and we are called to communicate it in ways that it can be understood. Note that Jesus called the fishermen to be *fishers of people*, not shepherds of flocks. He talked to them in terms they understood from their own experience. Of course the disciples likely *knew* what a shepherd was, but none of the fishermen had *been* shepherds, a fact that would have made a call to shepherding, however intriguing, difficult for them to imagine and accept. The fishermen had been fishermen all their lives, so Jesus put his invitation in language that resonated with their experience. Dramatic communication is the water we float in: Jesus wants to get in it with us. That's the invitation.

WHAT'S A SKETCH?

A sketch is a short, focused drama. As with visual art, a dramatic sketch is meant to convey not every detail of a scene but rather its overall shape, something outstanding about it, a single detail, a way or moment of seeing. A portrait-artist friend of mine often does several sketches of a person before she paints the complete portrait in oil on canvas. The sketching process helps her see her subject from many perspectives. She often notices things she would not otherwise have seen: the way a person's hand drapes on the sofa, or a strand of hair out of place.

Dramatic sketches do the same thing for the audience. They offer a view that helps us think about the whole, often in a new way. Sketches are different from skits, which are those things you do for talent night at camp. A sketch is meant to evoke and provoke. It's not made just to be funny or to draw attention to the performers. It neither lays it all out there like a play nor informs like a sermon. Sketching is an art form of its own within drama.

This book includes sketches that were written for and used in worship, outreach and other performance settings to engage the audience in exploring a story. They were not written as complete plays. The stories do not always include the entirety of a passage of Scripture. They don't generally quote the passage. Locations, names and historical periods have been changed.

If you've been in Christian circles much, you know that we tend to go flannelboard—to wrap our stories up with a nice, neat, flat ending so we know that God is good and the hero is okay at the end. But life isn't like that. It wasn't like that for the people described in the Bible. Even if we trust that God makes "all things work together for good" (Romans 8:28), we don't know ahead of time *how* he will accomplish that. We usually don't know how things are going to turn out; sketch characters shouldn't know ahead of time, either.

These sketches are written, with few exceptions, to be underplayed. That means the characters stick close to natural ground. Big gestures, sentimental line readings and overly emotional responses should be set aside. For example, rather than the actor having to *play* confusion ("Look at my face. See? I'm sooooo confused."), the script creates the *sense* of confusion in the actor's words. The audience should be able to identify *with* what the character is experiencing ("I've felt sad like that") without overtly identifying *what* the character is doing ("Oh, look, Suzanne is doing a really good 'sad' look right now"). The experience of the sketch comes through the words spoken by the characters. Trust the script. If it doesn't work, let me know.

We need to draw the audience into

the story. We want them to wonder. We want them to want more. I hope this book will help you create moments of wonder and wanting, and that over time and through experience your audience will find themselves, like the characters, wrapped up in the story of the Hero.

NOTES

[1]Dorothy L. Sayers, *Creed or Chaos?* (New York: Harcourt, Brace, 1949), p. 7.
[2]Murray Watts, *Christianity and the Theatre* (Edinburgh: Handsel, 1986), p. 2.
[3]Calvin Seerveld, *Bearing Fresh Olive Leaves* (Toronto: Toronto Tuppence, 2001), p. 36.

USING THIS BOOK

You are welcome to use these sketches for free public performance, provided

- a copy of this book is purchased for each actor;
- you credit this author and book as the source (in a program or on a screen).

Please do *not* copy these sketches and distribute them. That would be both illegal and unfair. Writers, including me, generally use the small amount they earn on books like this in order to write more—I promise I'm not raking it in and buying a yacht. Thanks for your partnership and respect in this matter.

If you would like to use one or more of these sketches for a paid performance (where you are being paid *or* where a ticket is charged), please contact the permissions department at InterVarsity Press (permissions@ivpress.com) to arrange for appropriate permission.

[Joseph] went to [Bethlehem] with Mary, to whom he was engaged and who was expecting a child. While they were there, the time came for her to deliver her child. And she gave birth to her firstborn son and wrapped him in bands of cloth, and laid him in a manger, because there was no place for them in the inn.

SELECTIONS FROM LUKE 2:1-21

1 WISH SOMETHING IMPORTANT WOULD HAPPEN AROUND HERE

A Sketch for Luke 2:1-21

This sketch is an unusual treatment of a Christmas text. Trust this script to make its point—that the kingdom of God shows up in our midst without flash—through the natural interactions of the characters.

Characters: SHARI, MARLA, PETE

Time: 2:40

Props: store items (cans, small boxes) to stack and move around; a counter or shelf on which to place them

SHARI *and* MARLA *work the night shift stocking shelves in a convenience store; elevator Christmas music plays in the background. They stack and move items as they talk.*

SHARI   So, how you doing?

MARLA   Pretty good. You?

SHARI   Oh, okay I guess. Been a little drab around here, 'specially for Christmas.
          It's different with the kids gone.

MARLA   Yeah. I can imagine.

Pause; they work.

MARLA   So, what're you doing for the weekend?

SHARI   Oh, I dunno. Donny and I sit in front of the TV a lot.

MARLA   You have favorite shows?

SHARI   I keep hoping there'll be a new Christmas special on or something, but I
          keep seeing the same ones as last year. Or maybe they all just look the
          same.

MARLA   Reruns, huh?

SHARI   What about you? Bet you're not watching much TV, with your new guy
          around. How's it going?

MARLA   Oh, it's nice. He's so great. I'll be glad when he's through grad school,
          though. The work is killing him!

SHARI   What's he working on?

MARLA   There's this new star he found. He's trying to track it or something.

SHARI   Wow. That sounds real important.

MARLA   Yeah, I guess. But then he has to write like a thousand pages about it . . .
          document, quantify, all that stuff. But yeah, it's pretty important.

SHARI   (*quietly*) I wish something that important would happen to me.

MARLA   Yeah. Be nice if anything important happened around here. I guess a star's better than nothing for a college town in the middle of nowhere.

Pause; they keep working for a moment.

MARLA   So . . . are the kids all coming home for the holidays?

SHARI   Yeah, they'll all be back for Christmas. I'm looking forward to it. Tom's getting married next year, so he'll bring his fiancée, plus Laurie and Matt will be back.

MARLA   That's nice.

SHARI   Yeah . . . I'm ready for these kids to get married, start having some grandchildren—My next-door neighbor, she has a new grandson.

MARLA   Oh, that's great. Have you seen him?

SHARI   Yeah. Cute little guy, no hair. But get this—her daughter and the boyfriend, they don't have money or jobs, so they had to move in with her parents. But the parents, they got two other kids still home, in high school, so they're in the garage.

MARLA   The daughter and the boyfriend . . . are living in the garage?

SHARI   Have the baby out there an' everything.

MARLA   Well . . . are they warm enough?

SHARI   Oh yeah, they set 'em up nice an' all. It's just that, you wish they'd've thought a little more, ya know.

MARLA   Yeah. That can put you in a bad situation, baby with no money.

SHARI   They'll figure out something.

PETE *enters.*

PETE   Hey, ladies.

SHARI   Hi, Pete.

MARLA   Oh, hi! *(hugging him)* How's it going tonight?

PETE   Well, it's pretty clear out, but I'm short on batteries for this one unit. Thought I'd stop by and stock up. What're you up to?

MARLA   Oh, not much important.

SHARI   Yeah, just working and talking. You know the drill.

PETE   Yeah, more or less.

MARLA   Shari's neighbor had a baby in the garage.

SHARI   And Marla told me 'bout your star. That's real exciting.

PETE   Yeah, I'm hoping. We keep finding out more about it.

SHARI   *(to herself)* Wish something important like that . . .

MARLA   *(overlapping SHARI)* We were just saying we wish something important would happen around here.

SHARI   . . . would happen around here.

PETE   *(laughing)* Yeah, I know what you mean. So which aisle for the batteries?

Fade.

Jesus, full of the Holy Spirit, returned from the Jordan

and was led by the Spirit in the wilderness, where for forty

days he was tempted by the devil.

LUKE 4:1-2

2 WISE UP

A Sketch Introducing Luke 4:1-13

The audience integrates these monologues, projected quotes and music in their own minds and hearts. Allow each character to have a different tone. The effect of very different characters sitting at the same desk, one after another, is quite striking. Temptation is a place we've all been.

Characters: MARTHA, TROY, LASZLO

Time: 8:00

Props: desk or table with chair and computer screen or laptop; phone; harmonica

Sketch begins with live or recorded playing of first verse and chorus of "Wise Up" (Aimee Mann, Songs from "Magnolia"). First four to eight bars play between each vignette. Three characters use the same desk and phone subsequently. A pinspot fades and comes up before each entrance. Quotes are projected on screen behind stage for each character and remain for duration of each monologue, changing at song. Song plays all the way through at close of sketch.

> PROJECTED ON SCREEN
>
> Over forty days, Jesus was tempted by the enemy in the wilderness, and he didn't eat anything. The enemy said to Jesus, "If you're the son of God, turn this stone into bread."

MARTHA *rushes to the phone, harried and frenetic. She speaks very fast.*

MARTHA   Hello, Julie . . . Marti calling—room parent things! Oh, yes, everything's fine. Jim will be out of the hospital in another two weeks . . . Well, the kids and I miss him, of course, but we're doing just fine. Thanks. How about you?

What's that? Bring over a casserole for us? Oh, that's so sweet of you to offer, Julie. Thanks, but we're okay . . . No, really. I've just juggled everything, you know . . . Yes, multitasking, the way of the world! . . . Yes, I'll let you know if I need help. But really, we're okay.

(quickly shifting into task mode) Okay, well, the reason I'm calling . . . to remind you about the school carnival . . . Yes, this Saturday . . . Billy and Jenna's class is responsible for the dunking booth and the fishing game and the bake sale . . . Well, I know it's a lot, but there wasn't anyone else who wanted to do it, so I volunteered. That's okay. I'm sure I'll find enough people . . .

The dunking booth? . . . Oh, that would be great. You can, uh, take the tickets . . . No, I've already arranged to pick it up myself . . . No, really, it's okay—I can pick it up on the way back from visiting Jim in the hospital . . . Really. Thanks for offering, though. You're so sweet . . .

Well, I've gotta go . . . But thanks for all your help. Thanks so much. 'Bye now.

Hangs up. Immediately picks up receiver and dials.

Hello, Mr. Abramian. Did that book come in? *Self-Sufficiency with Style and Prowess* . . . Yes, yes, it does sound helpful, doesn't it? . . . $17.99, right . . . Thanks. I'll be by tomorrow. Thank you so much.

Hangs up. Immediately picks up receiver and dials.

Hello, Aunt Priscilla. How are you, Auntie? . . . Good . . . Yes, we're fine . . . Well, Jim did have the surgery, but he's only in the hospital for two more weeks and then rehab will start . . . Yes, the kids and I miss him, but you know how it is—life goes on and on and on!

Well, I wanted to let you know that I'd be *happy* to host the family reunion . . . Yes, I think I can put some things together right away. En-

graved invitations, some home-cooked food, all the family favorites . . .
That's right! I'll be sure to hire an accordion player so Uncle Otto can
teach us all the chicken dance. Excellent idea . . . Oh, and a photogra-
pher, too, right . . .

Well, thanks for your concern, Auntie. I know, it seems like a bit to
handle with Jim out of commission, but I like to stay busy. Can never
be too busy. And this way I can do things just the way I like them. You
know what Great-Grandma Oberholtzer used to say, "If you want something done right" . . . Right! Yes, absolutely.

Okay, then. Well, I hope you and Uncle Otto are well. I'll call you in
the next couple of days to confirm the date and time. And the accordion
player. Love you. 'Bye.

*She hangs up, leans back in her chair, exhales deeply; gathers her resolve and claps her
hands. She gets up quickly and exits, still in frenetic mode, to get to the next thing.*

"Wise Up" plays.

PROJECTED ON SCREEN
The enemy led Jesus up and showed him all the kingdoms of the world in a moment
of time. The enemy said, "If you worship me, I'll give you all this domain, and power
and glory."

TROY *enters quickly and sits down at the desk. He places a phone call.*

TROY   *(formally, to an operator on the other end)* Hello, is Mr. Brightbill in,
please? Thank you.

(To the secretary on the other end) Hello, Judy. Is Bob in? Troy Lundy . . .

(under his breath to himself, bitterly) President of the Higgins County
Harmonica League—*(interrupted by greeting)*

Hey, Bob. Troy here. Yeah . . . Look, uh, Bob, we've gotta talk about this
merger. Well, ya know, it's just not what I was expecting. I mean, I just
think I have a right to expect that when you merge two organizations like
this, you know, the leadership oughta have more options, not fewer . . . No
. . . Well, I don't like that I've basically been demoted here . . .

Oh, sure, I keep my job, but I didn't keep the perks . . . *Presidents* deserve *perks*, Bob . . . What about the free tickets? I'm not staying in this organization without the free tickets, Bob. That's a non-negotiable . . . Do you know what those Higgins County Harriers games mean to me, Bob? Yeah, that's right. They're important, Bob. And another thing: the scooter. I gotta have the scooter, Bob . . . Well, I know you're trying to cut costs, but I mean, c'mon. That scooter gives me an aura, a presence . . . It says, "Hey, Troy's got a scooter, he's the man" . . . And I think the president of the biggest marching harmonica band in the county oughta have a presence . . . I keep the scooter, Bob. No scooter, no deal . . .

It's about presence, Bob . . . Look. I bought the harmonica. I practiced every day. I got good. I got *real* good, Bob. And I'm not letting some schmoozy merger with a pesky little banjo society like yours get in the way of my harmonica glory . . . That's right, Bob . . . And you'd better get outta my way, 'cause baby, I'm playin' and marchin' and no one's stopping me from running for state league president next convention. I'm on my way . . . You mark my words, Bob Sha-Bob . . . *(blowing harmonica into phone)*

Don't get in my way. And you can take your banjo and . . . and . . . and . . . and *do* something with it.

He hangs up and plays a bit, badly, on his harmonica; he gives himself a grunt of self-congratulation; he exits.

"Wise Up" plays.

> PROJECTED ON SCREEN
> The enemy led Jesus up to the top of the temple in Jerusalem, and said, "If you're the son of God, throw yourself down and see if the angels will catch you."

LASZLO *enters, sits at desk; he pitches a sale on the phone. Pinspot light comes up.*

LASZLO   Look, I'm trying to tell you how to do it right here, okay? What you wanna do is minimize risk . . . Right. You don't wanna put anything on the line if you don't have to . . . Right! You wanna be the biggest fish in the pond—by a long, long way, baby! You wanna be the biggest . . .

T. Rex, for sure . . . Uh-huh . . . Uh-huh . . . Riiiiiight . . . Yep . . . Uh-huh . . . Look, Rob . . . You're gonna be Tyrannosaurus Rob, dude . . . Now, let's look at those numbers, huh? . . . Right . . . You are so, so right . . . Safety in numbers . . . Okay.

(speaking quickly) I'm looking at going with 28,000 units of Mertz combined with 34,000 shares of Kornheiser . . . Then there's that Harger-Walsh-Lopez-Luten-Mastrogiovanni merger coming up . . . Nah, that's been all over the news . . . Keep the risk down, right . . . Keep the risk down, babe . . .

Okay, here are your other numbers: 14-5 via the sixteenth on 33 . . . Uh-huh. Then 95 thousand, right . . . Oh, exponentially! Absolutely. Then how 'bout 19,000 over 5 on the fifth percentile . . . right . . . Plus the potential . . . Uh-huh, very, very safe, Rob . . . That's a good one. 16. After that, there's a 15 percent risk. I know, I know . . . We need to get that risk down further, Rob, and we will . . . I know you're concerned for the future, Rob, and we'll do everything we have to do to make it work . . . On our way to risk-free investing . . . You know it! . . . We're positioned to keep your risk low . . . That's right, no firm does it better than Laszlo and Finnegan . . .

Well, what we do is, let's say you wanna buy 10 shares of MicroCom . . . *(laughing)* Right! Not that you would . . . What we can do for ya is . . . right . . . Then when you order a put . . . right . . . We buy in bulk—let's say, a hundred of MicroCom—right before we sell it for ya . . . and that drives up the price . . . Uh-huh . . . Buying lots of what you wanna sell . . . makes it more valuable . . . And then we can unload it later . . . Everyone ends up making buckets o'cash . . . It's beautiful, Rob. Just beautiful! It's like the Volvo of investing . . . Right—airbags everywhere, safest thing on the road . . .

Okay, you giant of the investing world . . . You're gonna be rich, man . . . You'll be able to retire on more than you ever imagined . . . Yeah, talk about your nest egg . . . Right, a dinosaur nest egg, for sure . . . You'll be the securest guy on the block, no doubt . . . That's right, Rob. It's all about safety . . . Your money, your investments, all safe . . . Right, that's what we're here for at Laszlo and Finnegan, to take the risks for you so you don't have to . . .

Okay, Rob . . . Tell Molly I said hi . . . Tell her that by the time she turns 30, we're gonna have you all set for life . . . It is a beautiful time to

be American, isn't it, Rob? . . . All right . . . See ya on Sunday, bro . . .
All right, have a great afternoon . . . Oh, you know it! Safest thing going.
'Bye.

He hangs up. Lights fade. As he exits, "Wise Up" begins; it plays in its entirety.

PROJECTED ON SCREEN DURING SONG
When the enemy had finished every temptation, he left Jesus until an opportune time.

Pause with this on screen, so people have a moment to reflect before moving on.

A Samaritan woman came to draw water, and Jesus said to

her, "Give me a drink."

JOHN 4:7

3 LAUNDROMAT—2 A.M.

A Sketch of John 4:3-26

This sketch is somewhat difficult to do. It *must* be underplayed; if the lines get too big, it will sound preachy. Remember that the characters onstage never act like they know they are part of the Bible. They experience the conversation as it happens, not from the perspective of being famous gospel characters.

Characters: MAN, WOMAN

Time: 4:30

Props: laundry basket with men's socks, boxers, t-shirts; half-full bottle of water; table and chair

It is 2:00 a.m. at the laundromat. WOMAN, alone in a pool of light, does laundry. She is tired—beat, really—and downcast. MAN approaches, weary.

WOMAN   *(curtly, not looking up from folding boxers, t-shirts, etc.)* Laundromat's closed.

MAN   *(dry throat, sweaty, and tired)* Uh, yeah . . . Do you know, is there a Coke machine in here or something? I've been walking the city; I'm parched.

WOMAN   What are you doing hiking around the city at 2:00 a.m. in the first place?

MAN   What are you doing in the laundromat at 2:00 a.m.?

Pause for her response of silence, like she could tell him but decides she won't.

WOMAN   *(after a long pause)* Look. There's no Coke machine here, and the laundromat, like I said before, is closed. See ya, bud.

MAN   *(seeing her bottle of water)* Could I have the rest of your water, there?

WOMAN   Look, buddy: I don't know who you think you are, but I don't even know you, and I'm not giving you my water. It's not like I can just go out and buy another one at this hour, and . . . You're just weird. You're creeping me out. So like I said before, in case you can't hear: The laundromat is closed. Buh-bye.

MAN   You have no idea who you're talking to, do you?

WOMAN   Oh, geez. Would you please just *go?*

MAN   If you knew anything about me, you'd be asking *me* for a drink, and I'd give you living water.

WOMAN   Of all the creeps wandering the city at 2:00 a.m., I get the creepiest. One more time: The laundromat's *closed.* The store's two miles down the road. If you want water—living, dead, whatever kind—you're gonna have to take a hike. Unless, of course, you can fly.

MAN   When you drink water, you get thirsty again.

WOMAN   *(snidely)* How insightful.

MAN   But anyone who drinks the water I've got: they'll never be thirsty. The water I give out turns into a spring that never stops gushing, and it makes you live forever.

WOMAN   They say if you talk to mentally ill people in terms of their reality, they'll calm down and leave you alone. So let's try this: *(facetiously)* Oh, gee! May I have some of the water you're talking about? Then I could avoid the long lines at the store, and maybe I would even have enough still gushing to do my laundry!

MAN   *(sitting)* Okay. Go call your husband and have him come down here.

WOMAN   To the laundromat?

MAN   *(leaning forward)* Uh-huh.

WOMAN   My husband. What's he gonna do? Help me fold laundry? *(pause; she is embarrassed and flustered; knowing she's cornered, she folds laundry with focus and fury, trying to figure out some way out of this shame trap)* Well . . . He—I mean, I don't . . . I don't have a husband. These *(referring to boxers, etc.)* are . . . They aren't my husband's.

MAN   You're right. You don't have a husband. You've had five husbands, and now you're living with a guy you're not married to. You told me the truth.

WOMAN   Um . . . What are you, like a preacher or something? How'd you know— wait. I remember a story about someone like you. I used to go to church, growing up. There was this guy who talked to some, um . . . some woman . . . Yeah, some lady, some woman . . . by a . . . well . . . Never mind.
        (pause; she reconsiders whether she wants to continue interacting; when she does, she becomes more strongly defensive) But I used to go to church, and I know about you religious types. You're always telling people about sin, how they're sinful, how bad and far from God we all are. *(accusatory; sotto voce)* Hypocrites.

MAN   Can I just tell you? The time is coming when people will come back to
           God. And they'll be . . . what they were made for . . . beautiful.

WOMAN   Yeah, I remember that stuff. *(picking up her laundry basket as a defense)*
           About a messiah coming and what he was gonna do—ride in on a horse
           and . . . And he's supposed to make everything new *(softening)* and right,
           or something. Good. How they were meant to be. *(sotto voce)* How . . .
           good.

MAN   Yeah, that's me. I mean, I'm him.

Music. (One good option is the song "You Split the Earth" by Delirious.)

WOMAN *looks at him like she's caught in headlights. Slowly recognizing what's happening, she lowers her laundry basket and puts it down, smoothes her hair, clears her throat, and backs toward the door.* MAN *touches her lightly, beginning a dance, and they turn 180 degrees (this is more warm than romantic).* WOMAN *then completes turn toward the door, starts to pick up basket; looks back at* MAN, *sets it back down because she doesn't need it, and rushes out . . .*

Out of pity for him, the lord of [a] slave released him

and forgave him [his ten-thousand-talent] debt. But that

same slave, as he went out, came upon one of his

fellow slaves who owed him a hundred denarii; and seizing

him by the throat, he said, "Pay what you owe."

MATTHEW 18:27-28

4 CHOPSTICKS

A Sketch of the Unforgiving Servant in Matthew 18:23-35

With my friend Daniel Jones, I was preparing a script about the unforgiving servant. We tried to think of the most insignificant thing two people would argue over to the point of unforgiveness. We improvised an argument, which I reworked into this sketch.

Characters: JACK, JANE

Time: 5:00

Props: a handful of chopsticks from a take-out restaurant, one broken in half; phone, couch

JACK *is on the phone, on the couch;* JANE *enters from side.*

JACK   So yeah, it was kind of unbelievable. Yeah . . . the officer, he pulls up behind me and I'm all scared and stuff. I mean . . . Yeah, you know I don't need a ticket, right? No joke. So anyway, he comes up to the window and does all his questions and stuff . . . Yeah . . . a construction zone. They *double* the fines. Yeah! 73 in a 40 zone. Ouch! . . .

       And then I, uh . . . Yeah, I try to explain, but it's not going that well, and he . . . Yeah . . . Uh-huh . . . Okay . . . Right . . . And then he says, "Well, today I'm not gonna issue you a citation. Today I'm gonna say, 'Drive a little more carefully and have a great day.' I'm forgiving the ticket." And so I'm all like, "Whoohoo!" I mean, what do you say? . . . Thanks, officer? I mean, it hardly seemed like enough to say, ya know? . . . Yeah, I know! Unbelievable. Dude let me off—I was completely grateful. . . . I know, who has that kind of cash to spend on *tickets?*

JANE *enters.*

JACK   Anyway, yeah, I should go . . . Yeah, Jane's here. . . . Alright. . . . Yeah . . . See ya later. 'Bye.

       Hey, Jane.

JANE *sits next to* JACK *on the couch.*

JANE   Hey. *(pause)* So, how're you doing?

JACK   Great. Just great. Got out of a ticket, so that's good.

JANE   *(nervously)* Oh, that's great. I'm really glad to hear . . .

JACK   So, what's up?

JANE   Well, uh . . . Actually, Jack, it's that I, uh . . .

JACK   You okay?

JANE   Yeah. It's just . . . Remember those extra take-out chopsticks you had, and I borrowed them yesterday?

JACK   Oh, yeah. That stockpile of the little ones, they come wrapped in paper.

JANE   Yeah, the ones left over from the last three years of take-out.

JACK   Well, what about them?

JANE   Well, um . . . I, uh . . .

JACK   Something wrong?

JANE   *(quickly spilling it as she pulls out the broken chopstick)* One of them broke. I don't know when, I don't know how . . . I'm really sorry, and I'll get you a new one. Sorry.

JACK   What?

JANE   *(holding up chopstick)* One of them broke. I'm sorry.

JACK   You broke my chopsticks?

JANE   One chopstick.

JACK   You're saying you *broke* one of *my* chopsticks?

JANE   Uh-huh.

JACK   Oh. My. Gosh.

JANE   I'm sorr—

JACK   *(interrupting)* You just broke one.

JANE   I don't think I actually broke it.

JACK   Well, then, who did, huh? Was it Santa Claus? King Kong?

JANE   I dunno. It was just like this . . . I went to gather them up to bring them back, all nice and washed, and this one was just . . . broken.

JACK   I can't believe this.

JANE   It's just a cheap chopstick, Jack.

JACK   It's *my* cheap chopstick, Jane.

JANE   I'm so sorry. But it's just take-out from the restaurant, right? I mean, we can get more—for free, even . . .

JACK   You wounded it. You . . . you hurt my chopstick.

JANE   Look. I didn't mean to. I'm sorry.

JACK   You think that matters?

JANE   I'm asking you: forgive me, please. And let me replace it.

JACK   Forgive you? You want me to *forgive* you?

JANE   Yeah.

JACK   What is wrong with you?

JANE   I . . . I . . .

JACK   What?! What is your problem? You waltz in here breaking my things and you think I'm just gonna forgive you? Well you've got another thing coming, honey. Forgive you my —

JANE   But Jack, it's a chop—

JACK   It was *my* chopstick. And *you* broke it!

JANE   I said I'd get you a new one!

JACK   I don't want a new one!

JANE   Well, I'll do whatever to replace it for you, to make it right.

JACK   Nothing is gonna make it right! You wrecked my chopstick! Now get out!

JANE   What? But you're my frien—

JACK   I said out! Chopstick wrecker!

JANE   I'd rather wreck a chopstick than a friendship.

JACK   Friendship, ha! I don't wanna be friends with you anyway. You always break my things! First my chopstick, then what? My coffee grinder? My, my—my Elvis statue? How 'bout my light-up vitamin reminder—you gonna break that too?

JANE   Okay . . . one more time: will you forgive me?

JACK   No! Just give me my wounded chopstick and get out!

JANE   *(stunned by* JACK'S *insistence, backs up slowly, handing off chopstick.* JACK *misses the pickup and it drops to the floor.)* Okay, but—.

JACK   I said GO! Get out! Out, out, out!

JANE   I'll wait for you to call and let me know when you're gonna forgive me.

JACK   That'll be a long wait, chopstick girl! *(he picks up damaged chopstick, twirls it, remembering to himself)* "Today I'm gonna say 'Drive a little more carefully and have a great day.'" Yes!

Zacchaeus . . . was trying to see who Jesus was, but

on account of the crowd he could not, because he was short

in stature. So he ran ahead and climbed a sycamore tree

to see him, because he was going to pass that way. When

Jesus came to the place, he looked up and said to him,

"Zacchaeus, hurry and come down; for I must stay at your

house today."

LUKE 19:2-5

5 GRAVITY

A Sketch About Zacchaeus in Luke 19:1-10

Bruce Kuhn came to perform his one-man *Gospel of Luke* for our church plant. I wrote this sketch as a prelude for the worship time, to help us focus on *why* we would want to hear the whole gospel, to give our attention to Jesus' story in Bruce's performance.

Characters: TWO ACTORS

Time: 3:30

Props: two ladders

TWO ACTORS *alternate lines, intermittently overlapping, while standing on ladders as high as safely possible.*

Note: They may move up and down the ladders as they wish. Try wrapping the ladders with light strings for an added effect.

So . . . when Jesus went around teaching . . .

When Jesus went around teaching, he taught crowds.

He taught such huge crowds

Really big crowds, it's true

People wanted to see him

To see him up close, to hear him—what was that like?

To hear him up close.

To hear and see him, face to face?

Do you ever wonder at it—

Do you ever wonder what it would be like

What would it be like?

To get that close to Jesus?

To see him up close?

To hear him right there?

To hear and see him right in the room—

To take him in full.

It must have been amazing, and I wish I could've been there.

I would like to have been there to see it.

To see and hear him myself.

To be there when people heard what they heard and saw what they saw.

Like that one time

There's that one time when Jesus walked through Jericho.

As he walked along the road through Jericho, and "Hey! Up there!"

Up in the tree—waaay up there—there was Zacchaeus.

Zacchaeus was so short, he couldn't see over the crowd.

And he was a tax collector—

Nobody liked him—

No one liked them because they stole money from their own people, pretty much.

That's why he was in the tree, hoping to see Jesus from a safe distance.

Jesus went walking down the street.

Jesus, like a rock star surrounded by fans.

So many people around him it was like a rock concert.

That's how much people wanted.

They wanted to hear Jesus.

They wanted to hear Jesus up close, right there.

They wanted to see Jesus face to face, to hear his voice.

They wanted to see him move, to have their ears filled by his words.

Zacchaeus wanted to hear Jesus.

Zacchaeus wanted to hear.

Zacchaeus climbed a tree, and waited.

And he waited.

And then Jesus showed up on the road.

And finally Jesus showed up—right there.

He stopped right under the tree.

He stopped right there—right under Zacchaeus.

Good thing Zacchaeus didn't lose a shoe up there.

Zacchaeus right above him.

If he'd dropped a shoe it would have hit Jesus square on the head.

He couldn't believe it.

There was Jesus, right up close.

As close as you could get to Jesus—in a tree.

And then—

Then, all of a sudden

Then Jesus—all of a sudden, he looked up

Suddenly Jesus looked up—right up.

And it was like something flew up instead of down and hit Zack on the head.

Jesus looked up, square at Zacchaeus, he looked up—thwack!

Like gravity reversed itself.

Like something—someone—pulled him up out of the tree.

Hey, Zacchaeus!

Jesus said, Hey!

Hey! Zack answered, jumping up, pulled down.

Hey, Zack! Come on down here!

Jesus called him. Come on down here! Hurry up!

I'm having dinner at your house.

Dinner at your place! Hurry! We gotta go!

Let's hang out at your house tonight. I'll come over.

Jesus is coming over to my house . . .

Zacchaeus never had people over.

To my house where people never come because they hate me.

No one much liked Zacchaeus—he was a tax collector and he was rich.

I have a rich house, but no one wants to hang out with me there.

Come out of the tree, Zack!

Jesus called him down.

Gravity turned around, and Zacchaeus, having gone up—

Jesus' words went up.

Zacchaeus came down.

He came down.

He came down and welcomed Jesus.

You're much taller than I'd imagined.

You're much shorter than is convenient.

What a sight to see up close, face to chest

Right there he welcomed Jesus, and they went to his house.

To see teacher and tax collector meet and walk . . .

They met and then they walked down that road.

Jesus still pursued, surrounded like a star . . .

God-as-guy come to meet stubby tax dude . . .

They stopped.

They stopped in the middle of the crowded path.

Zacchaeus said, I want to be so different.

I want to live differently, said Zack.

I want to give back what I stole.

I want to turn around.

Come out of the tree.

I want to give away, give it back and then some.

Live where people live.

Open my bags, let fly up and out and back.

I want out of the tree.

I want to be found.

Please find me.

See me up here?

Find me in this huge, rock star crowd.

I want to see Jesus.

I want Jesus to see me.

I want to hear his voice.

Up here, see me.

Carried up on gravity

I want my ears full of his words.

To see him myself

I wonder what it would be like to get that close to Jesus.

To take him in full

To hear him and see him right in this room

To expect him

To get Jesus face to face

To come down out of my tree

I want to see.

I want to turn around and see Jesus.

I want to hear.

I want to be here.

I want down.

I want to get close.

I want to hear Jesus call me down

I want to get Jesus.

Invite himself over for dinner

I want to hear what Jesus says.

To see what Jesus does . . .

I want down.

To be found with Jesus

I want to get found.

I want to hear from Jesus.

I want to see him face to face.

But first he has to find me.

Find me.

Find me.

No one after drinking old wine desires new wine, but says,

"The old is good."

LUKE 5:39

6 DEER BLANKET

A Sketch for Luke 5:39

Luke 5:39 has always intrigued me. It bespeaks the difficulty of the new: even when it's good, we have a hard time with change. My friend Aaron owned a truly hideous foam blanket with a picture of deer airbrushed on it. I mean, it was the worst! We often teased him about it, and when he became engaged to be married, we warned him of its demise: "Tracey is never gonna let you bring that into a new home!" The deer blanket now resides in the props box in my garage.

Characters: HANS, GUIDO

Time: 4:15

Props: blanket with deer print *or* other odd bachelor's item (a stuffed squirrel, an old football helmet, an ugly pillow); at least one large jar of animal crackers; several boxes of macaroni and cheese (some empty, some new); dirty socks; a jar of peanut butter; a nearly empty bag of chips strewn about but within reach of the actors

Note: Other (stereotypical) bachelor pad items may be added: for example, old pizza boxes, a CD player and open CD cases, a flag, pillows, and a full laundry basket. If you use something other than a deer blanket, adjust language throughout.

HANS *and* GUIDO *sit on an old couch in their apartment—a shabby, ill-kept bach-elor pad. An ugly foam blanket printed with a picture of deer is draped over the back of the couch, close enough for* GUIDO *to grab it.*

HANS   *(entering)* Dude, I'm so hungry. Hand me the peanut butter, will ya?

GUIDO   Uh . . . I think we're outta bread. *(looking around)* We got animal crack-ers, though.

HANS   Eew. They're, like, little *bears*. Where'd you get those?

GUIDO   Heather brought them over.

HANS   Never mind the peanut butter. Just send over the chips.

GUIDO *hands bag of chips to* HANS.

HANS   *(looking, finding mostly crumbs)* What's left of them, anyway . . . So, how was your weekend?

GUIDO   It was . . . It was good, I guess.

HANS   Yeah, great. I thoughta you out on the trail yesterday. Geez, it was beau-tiful. Just me and my pack and all of nature. Very, very cool. You should try it some time, Guido.

GUIDO   Yeah, well . . . See, I've been wanting to talk to you about something.

HANS   You wanna go with me next time? That'd be great! Just two guys and their packs and all of nature. Sure! You can come. How 'bout in two weeks?

GUIDO   It's not that, Hans, but thanks for the invitation. It's something else.

HANS   What? What is it?

GUIDO   Umm . . .

HANS   You can tell me, bud. C'mon. We've been roommates for . . . What is it, like, three years? You sick? *(imagining)* Is it your mom or something? *(sympathetic)* Do you need money?

GUIDO   No . . . It's just that . . .

HANS   Guido, come *on.*

GUIDO   Okay. *(breathing deep; speaking very fast)* I'm thinking about marrying Heather.

HANS   I'm sorry, Guid, I guess I was crunching too loud on the chips and I didn't really hear you. It sounded like you just said "marrying."

GUIDO   I did.

HANS   You did?

GUIDO   I'm thinking about asking Heather to marry me, Hans.

HANS   Heather? . . . You?

GUIDO   We've been going out for four years, and we've had time to think it over and pray about it and stuff . . . I think she's the one, Hans. I'm in love.

HANS   You're in love.

GUIDO   Yep.

HANS   Well . . . Ya know, that might be good. Wow. I need to think. *(to self)* Think fast.

GUIDO   Hans? Are you okay? I mean, I want you to be in the wedding and everything. And we'll still totally hang out and stuff. It'll be just like old times, like now.

HANS   (*re-engaging* GUIDO; *speaking as though in trance*) It will never be the same.

GUIDO   Sure it will! We can still go on that hiking trip. Promise! Just us and our packs and all nature.

HANS   It will never be the same.

GUIDO   Okay. Maybe it won't be quite the same.

HANS   You'll have to do your laundry.

GUIDO   Laundry? I already do that.

HANS   You'll have to do it before you run out of clean boxers.

GUIDO   Okay, okay. Laundry. Big deal.

HANS   You'll have to take out trash.

GUIDO   Yeah, I guess we actually kind of need to do that here, huh? But . . . So?

HANS   You'll have to eat meals.

GUIDO   Dude, I can't wait. Heather and I really like to cook together, you know?

HANS   Her Aunt Doris will give her a casserole recipe book. She'll want to try making all the casseroles.

GUIDO   Casseroles. I can handle that.

HANS   Oh? Can you handle budgets? Fighting someone for blanket coverage? Picking up your dirty socks off the floor every single day of your life? (*fearfully sanctimonious*) 'Cause other people's dirty socks, and their dirty diapers, and playdates at the gnat-infested playground, and carpools, and girl stuff in your laundry, and still fighting for the covers at night . . . And by the way, what if she *snores*? Huh, Romeo? *Then* whatcha gonna do? Huh?

(impassioned) It will *never be the same.* The old ways, the time-honored and sacred traditions of bachelorhood will be gone. Gone, I tell you. Just —gone.

GUIDO   Wow. Well, now thatcha put it *that* way . . .

HANS   *(sincere)* I'm telling you this for your own good, buddy.

GUIDO   *(wistful)* I might really miss it . . . Macaroni and cheese with extra Cheez Whiz. The freedom not to shower . . . Making sculptures out of the dirty socks.

HANS   Not to mention the deer blanket.

GUIDO   The deer blanket will always be with me. I love the deer blanket.

HANS   It's gonna have to go, Guido. No woman is gonna let that thing in her living space.

GUIDO   It's my deer bla—

HANS   *(cutting him off)* It smells like beer, Guido. Remember the first time you brought Heather over here, when we first moved in? And she said it smelled?

GUIDO   Well, I had it cleaned, and it—

HANS   It's not gonna make it, Guido. The deer blanket's goin' down, buddy. It's over.

GUIDO   I never thought—

HANS   No one ever thinks about it. It's too frightening. New things . . . They're just not like the old things, ya know?

GUIDO   Old things . . . like my deer blanket.

HANS   *(right on his heels)* Like the deer blanket. That's right. Now, are you *sure* you wanna marry Heather?

GUIDO   I . . . I dunno.

HANS   Think it over, friend. Think it over.

GUIDO   I . . . I guess I'll sleep on it, or something.

HANS   That's it. Take your time. Those big life transitions are to be approached slowly and carefully, pal.

GUIDO   Yeah . . .

HANS   Hey! I know! Ya wanna make some macaroni and cheese?

GUIDO   And we can have animal crackers dipped in peanut butter for dessert!

HANS   Bachelorhood . . .

GUIDO   Hard to beat, isn't it?

They sit down and begin to open a box of macaroni and cheese. Fade.

Why do you see the speck in your neighbor's eye, but do not notice the log in your own eye?

LUKE 6:41

7 ETHEL AND MYRTLE HAVE A SOCK

A Sketch of Luke 6:41-42

Ethel and Myrtle, recurring characters originally created for two college friends, have a delicious way of illustrating Jesus' teaching.

Characters: ETHEL, MYRTLE

Time: 2:00

Props: two laundry baskets; assorted laundry; one sock, taped to ETHEL's shirt

ETHEL *and* MYRTLE *fold clothes at the laundromat. Each is occupied with her own work; they talk but don't initially pay much visual attention to one another. ETHEL is adorned with a sock, stuck to her shirt, which she does not notice.*

ETHEL　　Lovely day, isn't it, dear?

MYRTLE　Why, yes, dear, it is. Quite nice. Are you making good progress on your laundry? *(turns to face* ETHEL *more squarely)*

ETHEL　　Oh, yes. It's nearly finished. And how are . . . *(looks up at* MYRTLE*)* Oh, dear.

MYRTLE　What? What's the matter?

ETHEL　　Well, dear . . . You have a piece of . . . lint.

MYRTLE　I do? Oh, goodness gracious, where is i— *(pause)* Oh, dear.

ETHEL　　What? What is it?

MYRTLE　Well, dear . . . *(giggling)* You have—

ETHEL　　Darling, the lint.

MYRTLE　Yes, yes, the lint. It's just that—

ETHEL　　Whatever the case, dear, you've got lint, right—

MYRTLE　But Ethel, dear, you've got *(laughing)* a—

ETHEL　　Dear Myrtle, I don't know what is so funny, but darling, you've got that lint fragment stuck on your—

MYRTLE　Yes, I know, Ethel, but you've got a—

ETHEL　　What? I've got a what?

MYRTLE　A sock! *(laughing uncontrollably)*

ETHEL　　Of course I have a sock. When you do laundry, you'll have the socks. Why is that so funny?

MYRTLE   *(sputtering it out through laughter)* Sock . . . on . . . you!

ETHEL   Well, yes, I am *wearing* socks, but I don't see why that is so funny. Myrtle, dare I say you are being either silly or cruel. Please calm yourself. And would you *puleeze* remove that terrible lint particle? It's really marring your style, my dear. You must do something about it. Mustn't leave ourselves linty. Linty, linty, linty—looks frumpy and unkempt. Calm down and remove that lint, if you would.

MYRTLE   *(attempting to regain composure)* Yes, yes. I'm sorry. It's just that you have a *(bursting again)* a . . . a . . . *sock!*

ETHEL   I have a sock.

MYRTLE   A sock!

ETHEL   A sock, you say. When all the while you're standing there with a piece of lint stuck to you. That is some nerve you have, accusing me of having a sock when you're practically covered with lint.

MYRTLE   *(still laughing)* Sock . . . is . . . so . . . big!

ETHEL   I see, Lady Lint. So, where is this sock?

MYRTLE   *(pulling herself together)* Ethel, you have a giant sock stuck to your front. A sock, dear. It's a sock.

ETHEL   *(finding sock; embarrassed)* Well, why didn't you tell me? What kind of friend are you?

MYRTLE   I was tryi—

ETHEL   *(grabbing her laundry basket to leave)* I have a mind never to do laundry with you again.

MYRTLE   But I tried to tell y—

ETHEL   *(hurt and indignant)* Well, you *didn't* tell me, and I had a sock stuck to
          me, and I looked silly. *(getting self-righteous)* And you, Myrtle Krabmeier,
          you still have a piece of lint.

Just then there came a man named Jairus, a leader of

the synagogue. He fell at Jesus' feet and begged him to

come to his house, for he had an only daughter, about

twelve years old, who was dying. . . .

Now there was a woman who had been suffering from

hemorrhages for twelve years; and though she had spent all

she had on physicians, no one could cure her.

LUKE 8:41-43

8 DAUGHTER

A Sketch of Luke 8:40-56

What was life really like for the people described in Luke 8:40-56? One daughter is known by her father's name and status; the other daughter isn't given a name at all. But Jesus heals both of them. How did getting well affect them? their families? Two women had intertwined lives but probably never knew each other.

Make sure you underplay this; otherwise it will be melodramatic. Keep the pace up; it's fine for lines to overlap a bit (some lines are marked to overlap). Think about how you would actually tell this story to some friends if you were your character.

Characters: JAIRUS, WOMAN, JAIRUS'S DAUGHTER

Time: 4:00

Props: none

Actors face audience, to whom they tell their interwoven stories. Actors may sit or stand. Try using levels to create a stage picture of the social and justice dynamics of this story.

JAIRUS   Jesus and the rock star crowd . . .

WOMAN   The crowd that followed him . . .

JAIRUS   The people who looked for him . . .

WOMAN   Looked to him . . .

DAUGHTER   Looked for him . . .

JAIRUS   Searched—they ran after Jesus searching . . .

WOMAN   Hoping . . .

JAIRUS   They needed what he had.

WOMAN   They followed Jesus, looking and searching and hoping.

Shift to active storytelling.

JAIRUS   It was a Tuesday.

DAUGHTER   I was twelve years old. It was a normal day.

JAIRUS   We were eating breakfast, and all of a sudden . . .

DAUGHTER   All of a sudden I felt . . .

JAIRUS   She got faint—she was burning up and then clammy and—

DAUGHTER   I don't know what happened. Really, it was all so fast. I got so sick . . .

JAIRUS   Something was wrong. We called the doctor, and he came out, and—It was so bad. He said . . . he said . . .

DAUGHTER   He said it was really bad.

JAIRUS   God, it was bad. He said it was really bad and she probably—

DAUGHTER   The doctor told them I wasn't gonna get better.

JAIRUS   I mean, what do you do? There had to be . . .

DAUGHTER   I mean, my dad is trying to figure out what could he do, and I guess he had heard this guy Jesus. He'd heard of him from other pastors around, or something, and—

DAUGHTER   *(together)* Supposedly he could heal people.

JAIRUS   *(together)* I had heard Jesus could heal people.

WOMAN   *(together)* I'd heard he could heal people.

JAIRUS   So I ran to the middle of town. He was there! I ran up and I . . .

WOMAN   I'd been looking for him, you know. I heard things and I was so sick and I . . .

DAUGHTER   So he ran out, looking for Jesus—I guess hoping he could do something.

WOMAN   I wanted him to do something.

JAIRUS   Jesus, I need you at my house. My daughter—Please, can you just come fast?

DAUGHTER   So my dad asked him to come right away.

WOMAN   It felt like forever. I had been sick for—I don't know, twelve years.

DAUGHTER   He said, "My daughter, she needs you, fast."

WOMAN   And I was hoping, maybe I would get better. Maybe it would stop if I could just . . .

JAIRUS   If Jesus could just come to the house, I thought, you know, he
              could do something.

WOMAN   If I could just maybe touch . . .

DAUGHTER   But I kept getting hotter and sicker . . .

JAIRUS   He said he would come—we could go to the house. So we went.

WOMAN   If I could reach just his clothes—just the edge of his shirt—maybe
              that would be enough, and no one would know, and . . .

JAIRUS   And then Jesus . . . stopped. He just stopped. We were going, and—

WOMAN   And it was.

JAIRUS   (together) He just stopped.

WOMAN   (together) It just stopped.

DAUGHTER   (together) My heart stopped.

WOMAN   The bleeding, it stopped—twelve years, stopped.

JAIRUS   He stopped in the road.

DAUGHTER   They stopped, and Jesus said, "Who touched me?"

JAIRUS   Who touched you? There were hundreds of people around him,
              and he's asking, "Who touched me?"

WOMAN   He said, "I felt it. Who touched me?"

JAIRUS   I was afraid . . .

WOMAN   Oh, God! What if . . . I didn't want anyone to see, to know. I
              thought . . .

JAIRUS	I thought we were going to my house—to my daughter.
WOMAN	I thought I would just touch . . .
JAIRUS	Who's not touching you?!
WOMAN	I did it. I touched you.
JAIRUS	What?—
WOMAN	I touched you, and it stopped.
JAIRUS	This sick, dirty woman came up and said, "I touched you."
DAUGHTER	And they stood there talking about it all.
JAIRUS	Then they sent word: she was dead.
DAUGHTER	And I was dead.
WOMAN	It stopped, and I could . . .
JAIRUS	My daughter's dead.
WOMAN	Have . . . a life . . .
JAIRUS	I couldn't hear the words . . .
WOMAN	I remember his exact words. He said . . .
JAIRUS	Jesus was talking.
WOMAN	He said, "Daughter, your faith rescued you."
JAIRUS	You had a chance to save her . . .
WOMAN	"Go in peace," he said.

JAIRUS   You could have rescued my little girl!

DAUGHTER   They planned a funeral.

JAIRUS   But you didn't and she's dead!

WOMAN   Then he kept going down the road.

JAIRUS   My daughter is dead.

WOMAN   Daughter. It was over, just like that.

JAIRUS   Daughter?!

DAUGHTER   It was over.

JAIRUS   I had a daughter, but she's dead. I came to you for help, with my
              daughter. And now what are you gonna do?!

DAUGHTER   But Jesus came anyway.

JAIRUS   What're you gonna do for a dead girl?

WOMAN   I'm well. Daughter, your faith made you well.

JAIRUS   He insisted, so we went. We got there and they were getting the fu-
              neral together.

DAUGHTER   All these people from church brought over food.

WOMAN   I thought about all the people I'd missed, all the life I hadn't been
              around for.

JAIRUS   And Jesus walked right into the middle of the whole thing and said,
              "She's not dead."

WOMAN   It was like I had come back to life . . . or something.

DAUGHTER   He said, "She's just asleep."

JAIRUS   People laughed. She was dead.

WOMAN   My old friends didn't even recognize me.

DAUGHTER   They knew I was dead.

JAIRUS   They knew.

WOMAN   They didn't know who I was.

DAUGHTER   I mean, I was cold and gray.

JAIRUS   He took us up to her room . . . She was so still . . . and cold . . . She was . . .

DAUGHTER   I mean, I *was*.

WOMAN   I was never there; life happened without me.

JAIRUS   She was . . . She wasn't there.

WOMAN   They didn't know what to do, seeing me.

DAUGHTER   They came in, and I guess Jesus said some stuff.

JAIRUS   He told us, "She's asleep, and we're gonna wake her up."

DAUGHTER   And I don't remember it, but . . . Well, what I do remember is this: I thought, *How cold . . . How cold I am, and it's so . . . dark.* Then I feel warm air moving over my face, and I hear someone . . .

JAIRUS   Jesus stood over her, just like it was morning, and said, "Little girl: Get up."

DAUGHTER   Get up, little girl.

JAIRUS   Get up.

WOMAN   Because of him . . .

DAUGHTER   And I opened my eyes . . . And it was him.

JAIRUS   It . . . was . . . her.

DAUGHTER   It was him. And he smiled, and my mom cried, and my dad hugged
              Jesus for about fifteen minutes.

JAIRUS   It was her. My daughter, awake, alive . . .

WOMAN   It was Jesus—he made me well.

DAUGHTER   I was all better.

JAIRUS   Jesus told us to give her something to eat.

WOMAN   I could get back to life.

DAUGHTER   All those people were still downstairs with the funeral food.

JAIRUS   So we took all the food people had brought and . . .

WOMAN   I wanted to throw a party or something.

DAUGHTER   So instead of having a wake, we had a party.

JAIRUS   We had a party.

DAUGHTER   The best party.

JAIRUS   A party for my daughter, who's alive.

WOMAN   I can have . . .

DAUGHTER   Alive.

WOMAN   A life.

A woman named Martha welcomed [Jesus] into her

home. She had a sister named Mary, who sat at the Lord's

feet and listened to what he was saying. But Martha was

distracted by her many tasks.

LUKE 10:38-40

9 SNACKS FOR JESUS

A Sketch of Luke 10:38-42

Sometimes a little twist, such as imagining sisters Mary and Martha instead as brothers Mario and Marty, can wake up a story that we've all heard before.

Characters: MARIO, MARTY, JESUS

Time: 2:30

Props: kitchen equipment such as mixing bowls, spoons, a tray, spatula, hot pads; some snack foods that can be stacked

Note: A little flour to puff up around MARTY can be a nice touch.

MARIO *enters kitchen as* MARTY, *his brother, is preparing food.* MARTY *wears an apron;* MARIO *wears scruffy clothes.*

MARTY   D'you get the yardwork finished, bro?

MARIO   Yeah. I put in a couple more tomato plants and that Japanese maple. And weeded. And put up the rabbit fence. Ya know, while I was out there I thought of, like, thirty things I wanna ask Jesus while he's here. D'you think of anything you wanna ask him about? Y'know, like gravity? Love? Biology? Sex?

MARTY   What about mowing?

MARIO   Mowing? That's kind of a dumb question.

MARTY   Dude, Jesus is coming over. Mow the lawn.

MARIO   Who cares how long the grass is?

MARTY   I care. Look, how often do you have Jesus in your *house?* Dude, this is important.

MARIO   Dude, Jesus made the grass.

MARTY   So?

MARIO   He's the grassmaker. I mean, he knows how high it gets.

MARTY   Well, Jesus is the weedmaker too, but you still pulled the weeds.

MARIO   True.

MARTY   Look, can you finish out there and then come back in quick and help me finish the snacks?

MARIO   Snacks for Jesus?

MARTY   Well, yeah. I mean, it's Jesus. You gotta have snacks.

MARIO   Mmm . . . Looks good. *(reaches for food)*

MARTY   They're for Jesus *only!*

MARIO   Whatever. Back in a few.

Doorbell effect or knocking.

MARIO   Oh, wait! That's probably him!

MARIO *exits to answer door;* MARTY *furiously attempts to finish snacks.*

MARTY   Oh, geez! Willya look at this?! I'm never gonna finish this in time! *(beat)*
         Hey, Mario!

MARIO   *(from offstage)* Yeah?

MARTY   Can you give me a hand in here?

MARIO   Sure, yeah. Hold on.

MARTY *continues to stack, stir, etc. He becomes progressively more agitated.*

MARTY   Yo, Mario!

MARIO   *(offstage)* What?

MARTY   Can you get in here?

MARIO   Sorry, sure. Yeah. I'm talking to Jesus. I'll be there in a sec.

MARTY   *(banging pots & pans; speaking to himself in mocking anger)* Oh, fine.
         You're talking to Jeeesus. How nice for you. And I'm stuck in this kitchen
         making snacks all day while you're off in deep, meaningful theological
         conversation. Well, someone has to do the catering around here, and I
         guess that's me. Snacks for Jesus coming *(bang)* right *(bang)* up *(bang)*!
         Geez—

JESUS *enters with* MARIO.

MARTY   —us! Jesus! Hey! Great to see you.

JESUS   Yeah . . . Everything okay in here?

MARTY   Well, you know I was just trying to get some help from my brother over
          there. I mean, he didn't mow the lawn, and the snacks aren't done, and
          you were coming over, and I just wanted stuff to, ya know, be cool. For
          you.

JESUS   *(pause, just long enough to make* MARTY *uncomfortable)* Yeah, okay. So
          . . . Is there a coffee shop or something around here?

MARIO   Yeah, a couple of them.

JESUS   Cool. How 'bout I take you guys out, we'll have some coffee, and we can
          just, ya know, sit and talk? I mean, dude, we only have so much hang
          time, and you're spending it all in the kitchen?

MARTY   *(all nice)* Right. Sure, okay. *(agitated, aside to* MARIO*)* What're we
          gonna do with the snacks? I made the snacks for Jesus!

MARIO   *(aside to* MARTY*)* It's cool, bro. Just . . . We'll, like, store them for later.
          Maybe he'll come over with all the disciples and we can have, like, a Jesus
          Party or something. Relax, okay?

MARTY   *(grudgingly)* I'll try *(trailing off as he crosses to exit)* But . . . The snacks . . .

JESUS   *(as they exit)* The yard looks great, guys.

MARTY   Yeah, although sorry the grass is so long. Oh, and there's some weeds still
          over there, where Mario missed.

JESUS   You know I'm the grassmaker, right?

MARIO   Weedmaker too.

JESUS   Absolutely. Weeds, grass. I've always liked how grass grows so high . . .

[Jesus] cried with a loud voice, "Lazarus, come out!" The

dead man came out, his hands and feet bound with strips of

cloth, and his face wrapped in a cloth. Jesus said to them,

"Unbind him, and let him go."

JOHN 11:43-44

10 SMELLY

A Sketch Introducing John 11

The raising of Lazarus from the dead is familiar, but what would it *really* be like to see someone walk out of a tomb? Can you imagine? And how about the formerly dead person's reintegration into daily life?

I wrote this for a South Philly accent, but you can do it straight. If it works better for your team, you can substitute Joe (a man) for JoJo.

Characters: LARRY, JOJO, TAMMY

Time: 4:20

Props: three fast food bags and cups; table and chairs or a counter set

Two people sit at a fast food counter eating their meals. A third person, LARRY, *approaches them from behind.* JOJO *and* TAMMY *smell him and react before seeing him.*

JOJO   Yo, what's that smell? Tammy, youze smell that smell? Wow! That's
            smelly!

TAMMY   Wow! Youze not kidding! That's some smelly smell I'm smelling!

JOJO   What could that be?

TAMMY   Geez! It smells like a rotten peach covered with vinegar and cooked over
            burning tires.

JOJO   No, no . . . It smells like a skunk with banana bubble bath poured over it
            and then left in the fridge for, like, three weeks.

TAMMY   That's disgusting!

JOJO   That smell is disgusting! Man, that's one bad smell. Grrrroooooooss.

TAMMY   But wha'do youze really think it is?

LARRY   Hey, girls. Bet youze didn't expect to see me here.

JOJO   Larry! Long time not seen! How ya been? Oh, Larry, this is my friend
            from the bowling league, Tammy. Tammy, my old friend Larry. So . . .
            Larry, what's youze been up to?

LARRY   (with studied nonchalance) Oh, gettin' raised from the dead.

JOJO   (assuming it's a joke) Yeah, cause that's what youze smell like, sweetheart.

TAMMY   Yeah. I mean, no offense and all, but youze do kinda smell . . . unusual,
            I guess.

LARRY   Well, it ain't no joke. I was dead. About twelve hours ago. In fact, this is
            my first foray back into the world of the living.

JOJO   Yeah, yeah. Cut the goofin' and tell me what really happened. Youze get
            sprayed by a skunk or what? Youze out huntin' again and got sprayed?

Remember when that happened to Ken last year?! Geez, he stunk like crazy for a whole week. Kept taking tomato juice baths, didn't do him a lick of good.

TAMMY   He deserved it, hunting down those innocent skunks.

LARRY   *(beat)* I was really dead. Yesterday.

JOJO   C'mon, Larry, I said cut the cow patties.

LARRY   I'm serious. Dude, I was so dead. Like a doorknob. Or a door. Or a window—or whatever. I was definitely dead, okay?

TAMMY   Youze were actually dead? No kiddin'?

LARRY   Nope, no kiddin'. Doggie-door dead. I was lyin' there, and it felt kinda cold—and real, real dark, like the haunted mansion at Disney World.

JOJO   Dude, that's a scaaary one.

LARRY   'Cept . . . Girls, this was real. So, like I was sayin', it was real cold and dark, and spooky-like. And I hear this voice off in the distance, going, "Larry! Larry! Come out!" And I'm like, "Come out of where?" Because I don't know where I am. . . . Maybe I'm at Disney and I just forgot. I dunno.

TAMMY   So did youze come out?

LARRY   Well, I came out in a minute, but I'm lyin' there and I'm thinking, *I should come out. I think I know that guy's voice.* But then I start to move and I can't move! There's these little white cloths all over me, like someone teepee'd me or somethin'. I dunno. But I can't move because these things are, like, tight. Like that mummy in . . . What's that movie, with that guy?

TAMMY   *The Mummy?*

JOJO   Oh, yeah. *The Mummy.* That's a scaaary one.

LARRY   Anyways . . . So I'm all wrapped up tight, but I hear this voice and I think, *That's my friend.* But I'm still sorta dead, so I think, *Why's he calling me now? I'm busy lyin' here.* But then I wake up, or life up, or whatever, and I realize I want to get up. So I kinda hoist myself upright, like this.

TAMMY   Ooh.

LARRY   And then I sorta walk out like this *(walks like a mummy)*, real stiff and all because I'm all in these little teepee things.

JOJO   Ooh, that musta been scaaary.

LARRY   A little. But then I hear my sister—you know my sis, Martha—Martha say, "Eeew. He's been dead four days. He's gonna stink-o!"

TAMMY   Turns out she was right.

LARRY   And I think, *I've been dead four days? Hardly seems like that long. An afternoon, maybe, but not four days. The time practically flew by.* I mean, one minute I was sick with a cold and whatnot, and the next minute I've been dead four days.

JOJO   Whoa. That is one amazing story.

TAMMY   And one amazing smell.

LARRY   Hey, gimme a break! I been dead four days. I mean, I showered and everything, but four days of rotting, decrepit tomb time, and it's gonna take a couple a showers to lose the scent—if youze know what I mean.

JOJO   I know what youze mean. Say, Larry, youze wanna join us here? *(flattering)* We'd be honored to have a formerly dead person dine with us. Youze must be famous, huh?

TAMMY   JoJo! He can eat with us only if we eat outside at a real big table with lotsa space.

JOJO   Yeah, okay. Youze wanna come outside and eat with us, Larry?

LARRY   Sure, that'd be great. Let's go.

They exit, imitating moments from LARRY's story and rehashing their conversation, laughing. In the midst of this, the following conversation fragment:

JOJO   *(filtering out as they exit)* So, Larry . . . Who was the guy?

LARRY   The guy?

JOJO   You know, the voice? *(imitating voice)* "Come out, Larry."

LARRY   Oh, yeah! That's the really interesting thing. You know, I didn't know he could do this, but . . .

They exit.

[The] master commended the dishonest manager because

he had acted shrewdly; for the children of this age are more

shrewd in dealing with their own generation than are the

children of light. And I tell you, make friends for yourselves

by means of dishonest wealth so that when it is gone, they

may welcome you into the eternal homes.

LUKE 16:8-9

11 THE TALE OF THE SHREWD MANAGER

A Sketch on Luke 16:1-9

This sketch is a bit campy, but Luke 16:1-9 is rarely studied, and the sketch tells the story pretty clearly, which is useful and fun.

Characters: SHREWD MANAGER, BEER-HAP-SABINA, BIG DEBTOR, LESSER DEBTOR

Time: 4:15

Props: hat, pink piece of paper, small bell

Note: The SHREWD MANAGER must be highly dramatic throughout and should use an affected British accent. Think of *Masterpiece Theater.*

Classical music plays.

SHREWD MANAGER   Welcome to Bible Theatre. I, the Shrewd Manager, wilt
                      be thine host for this evening's entertaining and quite the-
                      atrical Bible tale. And now, without further ado and
                      amen, we present, "The Tale of the Shrewd Manager,"
                      starring . . . me.

Stop music. He turns, returning with a hat to begin story.

SHREWD MANAGER   There I was, collecting minas, talents, baths, kors, shek-
                      els—you know, all those biblical kinds of money. There I
                      was, collecting biblical money, when Beer-hap-Sabina,
                      secretary to Lord Finance (that would be, to you post-
                      moderns, my *boss*) . . . Beer-hap-Sabina entered stage
                      right and delivered to me a most alarming notice. It was
                      pink, and a slip—yes, a pink slip.

BEER-HAP-SABINA   (*entering from side, dings small bell, hands* SHREWD
                      MANAGER *pink piece of paper*) Your pink slip, Sir
                      Shrewd Manager. (*dings small bell, bows and exits*)

SHREWD MANAGER   (*shuddering*) Oh, no! Not a pink slip! But (*shifting accents
                      to "Gone with the Wind" Southern*) where will I go, and
                      what will I do? I am of gentle breeding and cannot dig
                      ditches, and I'd be too terribly ashamed to beg. (*shifting
                      accents back to British*) Well my options are certainly lim-
                      ited, aren't they?

                          (*to audience*) It's at these moments when being the
                      Shrrrewd Manager—as opposed to your average duller
                      manager—is quite of use.

                          (*back to talking to self*) I know what I must do. I will use
                      this last day of labor to win for myself the most friends I
                      can, so that I might not dig nor beg, but might be wel-
                      comed into their estates to sponge off them as necessary.

BIG DEBTOR *enters.*

SHREWD MANAGER   Ah, my first opportunity. I shall be shrrrewd!

BIG DEBTOR   Good afternoon, Shrewd Manager. How are ya?

SHREWD MANAGER   I'm quite fine, thank you, Big Debtor. Say, how's that lovely payment plan working out for you? Are you able to make the payment due today?

BIG DEBTOR   Well, Shrewd Manager . . . You see, sir, I'm having a little trouble, and I can't pay until next week, and I was hoping you'd be able to give me a little leeway, sir, and—

SHREWD MANAGER   *(interrupting)* No bother, Big Debtor. I was merely asking because I'm running, shall we say, a bit of a *special* today. How much do you owe Lord Finance?

BIG DEBTOR   Uh, well, I guess about a hundred thousand . . .

SHREWD MANAGER   Well, take your bill and make it fifty thousand.

BIG DEBTOR   What? You can do that? You can just . . . like . . . make it fifty instead of a hundred? Whoohoo! Yipee yay! Why, thank you, Mr. Shrewd Manager! Say, if you ever need anything any time, y'all just let me know, all right? 'Cause you are one shrrrewd dude!

BIG DEBTOR *exits.*

SHREWD MANAGER   *(noting the audience, and shrewdly)* All right, I'll just let you know if I ever need anything, friend . . .
    (to audience) Ha! This truly works!
    (back to drama, with utmost dramatic flair) I shall be shrrrewd!

LESSER DEBTOR *enters.*

SHREWD MANAGER   Well, good afternoon, Lesser Debtor. And how are we today?

LESSER DEBTOR   *(listless, Eeyore-like)* Oh, Mr. Shrewd Manager, the hurricane wiped out my olive grove . . . And I have to have my wisdom teeth pulled . . . And I can pay only part of my bill to Lord Finance . . . And it's my birthday, but no one will remember . . .

SHREWD MANAGER   You mention part of a bill. How much do you owe, exactly? Let's see here, it says a thousand.

LESSER DEBTOR   Oh. A thousand . . .

SHREWD MANAGER   Let's make it . . . seven hundred.

LESSER DEBTOR   *(suddenly changing personality)* What? Only seven hundred? Well I've got six hundred right here! That means I'm almost paid up! Whoohoo! Yipee yay! Thank you, Mr. Shrewd Manager! You are so very shrrrewd! *(singing)* Happy birthday to me! Happy birthday to me! Say, Mr. Shrewd Manager, you know, if I can ever do anything for you, *(singing)* you just call out my name, and you know wherever I am, I'll come running . . .

SHREWD MANAGER   Yes, well, thank you, Lesser Debtor.

BEER-HAP-SABINA   *(entering, interrupting* LESSER DEBTOR'S *celebration; dings bell, hands* SHREWD MANAGER *another piece of paper)* Mr. Shrewd Manager, Lord Finance would like to see you immediately. He said something about irregularities in debt repayment?

SHREWD MANAGER   Uh, yes. *(to audience)* Lord Finance wants to see me. *(to Beer-hap-Sabina)* I'll be right in, then, Beer-hap-Sabina. Thank you.

BEER-HAP-SABINA *dings bell, exits.*

SHREWD MANAGER   *(turning to audience, removing hat)* Well, as you might imagine, I had quite a meeting with Lord Finance. You probably think I got quite a wrist slapping. But really, Lord Finance admired my shrrrewdness—and I shall be shrrrewd!—and sent me freely to the countryside to pursue a life of leisure, being welcomed into the finest estate houses in all the land. Not bad, really . . .

Well, that's all for this edition of Bible Theatre. I hath been thine host, Shrewd Manager, in this tale of . . . the Shrewd Manager. And now as we part, may all your days be biblical and all your nights be . . . Well, may all your nights be biblical, too. Amen and good evening.

Classical music. He exits.

[The women] found the stone rolled away from [Jesus']

tomb, but when they went in, they did not find the body. . . .

On that same day two of [the disciples] were going to

a village called Emmaus, about seven miles from Jerusalem,

and talking with each other about all these things that

had happened. While they were talking and discussing,

Jesus himself came near and went with them, but their eyes

were kept from recognizing him.

LUKE 24:2-3, 13-16

12 EMMAUS

A Sketch of Luke 24:1-32

This sketch explores two divergent experiences of Jesus' death and resurrection. Be sure to underplay it. The characters are recalling, looking back at the experience they had in the moment rather than having it right then.

Characters: CLEOPAS, JOANNA

Time: 5:00

Props: couch or stools for actors to sit on

CLEOPAS *and* JOANNA *tell their story to a third party (the audience) but conversationally, including one another in their telling and really telling it in tandem (think of the way long-term married couples or siblings tend to tell stories in tag-team fashion, jumping back and forth on one another's comments).*

CLEOPAS   She showed up at the door out-of-breath, she'd been running. "We went to the cemetery," she said.

JOANNA   We went to the cemetery. And it—

CLEOPAS   She said, "It's not there."

JOANNA   He's not there.

CLEOPAS   The body's not there.

JOANNA   We went to look for him.

CLEOPAS   They were looking for him at the graveyard.

JOANNA   We looked everywhere. He's not there.

CLEOPAS   Did you look everywhere?

JOANNA   At first we thought, *Oh, God, why would someone* . . .

CLEOPAS   Wasn't it enough they beat him up, thrashed him till he was . . .

JOANNA   Why—who *does* that?

CLEOPAS   He was like a shard, barely anything left.

JOANNA   They crucified him—now they stole him?

CLEOPAS   They crucified him—now the body was gone.

JOANNA   And we're thinking, *This is awful* . . .

CLEOPAS   We didn't know what to think.

JOANNA   Where did they take him?

CLEOPAS   We thought, *Well, they're probably just upset.*

JOANNA   What *is* this?

CLEOPAS   The three of them—

JOANNA   Then there were two of them, these . . . bright . . . men.

CLEOPAS   Then they saw two men—shimmering . . . people.

JOANNA   Oh, my God. This is . . . This is weird.

CLEOPAS   And we're thinking, *Well that's bizarre.*

JOANNA   This is too weird, we can't be seeing this.

CLEOPAS   They must be making it up.

JOANNA   They were scary—It was so bright—

CLEOPAS   You were afraid.

JOANNA   We thought maybe it wasn't real—it was in our heads.

CLEOPAS   But you all saw the same thing.

JOANNA   But it wasn't—It was two bright . . . guys.

CLEOPAS   We didn't believe them at first.

JOANNA   It was too bizarre.

CLEOPAS   But it did make me wonder.

JOANNA   They said—The bright guys said, Why are you here?

CLEOPAS   It made me think.

JOANNA   I mean, as *if* . . .

CLEOPAS   *(to* JOANNA*)* After all, you were there.

JOANNA   Why are you looking for a live person in a graveyard?

CLEOPAS   You saw it.

JOANNA   *(to bright men)* Why? *(beat—incredulous, angry)* Because they killed him!

CLEOPAS   *(to audience)* They crucified him, and we all saw it.

JOANNA   *(explaining)* His body . . . It . . . He . . . was dead.

CLEOPAS   We took him down.

JOANNA   He was cold . . . and gray . . . and so still . . .

CLEOPAS   He was gone.

JOANNA   *(to bright men)* He's—his body—is here.

CLEOPAS   Then his body . . . was gone.

JOANNA   They said, No, his body's not here. Remember? Remember, about rising? He told you he would rise the third day. He said he would be killed and come back in three days. *(beat—sotto voce, a secret reminder)* It's the third day.

CLEOPAS   It *was* three days.

JOANNA   His body's not here. He's not here.

CLEOPAS   Three days. He rose.

JOANNA   He's not here because he's not dead.

CLEOPAS   *(to* JOANNA*)* When you all came back and told us, He's not there, he's not dead . . .

JOANNA   *(to audience)* They killed him, but he got up and walked out.

CLEOPAS   *(to audience)* I didn't know what to do. How could that happen?

JOANNA   They didn't know what we meant.

CLEOPAS   You die, you die. Right?

JOANNA   *(to* CLEOPAS*)* You thought we were making this up?

CLEOPAS   *(to* JOANNA*)* Well, I remembered what he said, but . . .

JOANNA   But you didn't believe us until later.

CLEOPAS   Yeah. *(acknowledging false bravado)* 'Cause *we* understood how things really were.

JOANNA   Like we had left reality.

CLEOPAS   Or so we thought.

JOANNA   You weren't gonna listen to us.

CLEOPAS   But can you really blame us? I mean, this was weird.

JOANNA   So he had to come talk to you himself.

CLEOPAS   *(to audience)* We walked with him for miles and didn't even know it.

JOANNA   *(still to* CLEOPAS*)* And even then you didn't get it.

CLEOPAS   We should've guessed from how much Scripture he knew.

JOANNA   He laid out all this Scripture for you.

CLEOPAS   He knew everything; it was amazing how much of the Word . . .

JOANNA   *(to audience)* He explained everything that happened.

CLEOPAS   He connected everything—every event—to Scripture.

JOANNA   Connected all the dots . . .

CLEOPAS   We heard all the stuff he said, but it still didn't make sense.

JOANNA   *(to CLEOPAS)* Turned out you were a little slow connecting what he said.

CLEOPAS   We were so slow to recognize . . .

JOANNA   This string of bizarre events . . .

CLEOPAS   My heart was . . . slow, heavy . . . I didn't get it.

JOANNA   *(to audience)* They didn't get it.

CLEOPAS   Slow, sad. I mean, it was great to think about the Scripture, but . . .

JOANNA   *(to CLEOPAS)* So you finally got to Emmaus.

CLEOPAS   It was late when we got there.

JOANNA   And you talked him into staying over, since it was late.

CLEOPAS   And this is so amazing, we didn't see it coming . . .

JOANNA   You didn't even see it coming.

CLEOPAS   We sat down to eat.

JOANNA   *(to audience)* They sat down for dinner.

CLEOPAS   *(imagining this)* He picked up a loaf of bread. He picked it up and said a blessing. He blessed the bread and broke it. And then he gave it to us. *(beat—sotto voce)* It was him.

JOANNA   It was him.

CLEOPAS   It was him.

JOANNA   *(to CLEOPAS)* And you knew.

CLEOPAS   We knew.

JOANNA   You didn't get it.

CLEOPAS   We had no idea.

JOANNA   And then you did.

CLEOPAS   And then we saw.

JOANNA   Get it. Finally.

CLEOPAS   We knew.

JOANNA   We weren't crazy after all.

CLEOPAS   It was him.

JOANNA   *(to audience)* They saw him.

CLEOPAS   Just like the women did, we saw him.

JOANNA   Like we saw the empty grave.

CLEOPAS   We saw his hands around the bread.

JOANNA   Like we saw the bright guys.

CLEOPAS   We saw him break bread.

JOANNA   We heard he had risen.

CLEOPAS   We heard him talk.

JOANNA   Didn't we know?

CLEOPAS   Didn't our hearts burn up?

JOANNA   Didn't we expect?

CLEOPAS   Did we not hear those words?

JOANNA   Didn't we expect his words to be true?

CLEOPAS   We thought he was just some guy on the road.

Lines overlap to end.

JOANNA   We didn't expect *him*.

CLEOPAS   We didn't imagine him . . . beyond death.

JOANNA   We saw a body—that's all we imagined.

CLEOPAS   We expected death.

JOANNA   We went looking for him in death.

CLEOPAS   We expected death.

JOANNA   We looked for death.

CLEOPAS   We *expected* death.

JOANNA   *He* expected life.

CLEOPAS   We were thinking about his death.

JOANNA   We were looking for a corpse.

CLEOPAS   We were just trying to get to Emmaus.

JOANNA   We were looking for a body.

CLEOPAS   We were looking for a way to remember him.

JOANNA   We were trying to find his body.

CLEOPAS   We looked at his death.

JOANNA   We searched for a dead body.

CLEOPAS   We sought after death.

JOANNA   We looked for a corpse.

CLEOPAS   But he was looking for us.

JOANNA   But a living person . . .

CLEOPAS   He was looking for us.

JOANNA   We went to the graveyard.

CLEOPAS   Searched for us . . .

JOANNA   We scoured the cemetery.

CLEOPAS   Looking for him . . .

JOANNA   Looking for his body . . .

CLEOPAS   We talked all the way to Emmaus.

JOANNA   Trying to understand . . .

CLEOPAS   We wanted to get it.

JOANNA   We looked.

CLEOPAS   We looked.

JOANNA   And all that time . . .

CLEOPAS   We looked for him.

JOANNA   We looked for him.

CLEOPAS   We were looking for death.

JOANNA   He was looking for us.

Lines separate a bit.

CLEOPAS   We expected death.

JOANNA   And he expected life.

CLEOPAS   He looked for us.

JOANNA   Alive . . .

CLEOPAS   For us . . .

APPENDIX

Here are two conversations between a group of actors who work on college campuses and in postmodern contexts: Scott Brill, Jason Gaboury, Lisa Harper, Susi Jensen, Daniel Jones, Bruce Kuhn, Alison Siewert, Jenny Vaughn Hall and Nina Thiel. Many of these artists have participated in the theater portion of the Urbana Student Mission Convention. You may want to use this dialogue as a starting point for reflection and discussion with your drama team about what you value in your drama ministry.

PART 1
What Is Drama?

Susi: Drama is putting a story on stage for the purpose of giving an audience experience of authentic human reality, especially struggle.

Scott: Fundamentally, drama is art. Just like painting, sculpture, poetry, music. It's a place of connection to universal human emotions.

Nina: Drama is a performance by one or more people that tells a story, shows an audience something of life. It connects to an audience primarily *affectively*, through allusion.

Bruce: Good theater is *life parable*— a story we can enter into, believe is happening, learn from if only by experience. Story is the tool of master teachers; sharp tools do most of the work, without a lot of grunting and sweat from the user.

Daniel: It's storytelling. It's creating pictures. It's art. It's raising questions. It's linear and nonlinear, clear and abstract. It's open ended and fluid. It gives us glimpses into our own lives and tells our own stories through the stories onstage. It can be beautiful or grotesque. It can be laugh-out-loud, slap-your-knees funny or deeply sad. It can make you angry. If it's good it provokes response. It should stop you and cause you to look around.

Jason: Drama is the relationship that is created among actors, a script and an audience. That relationship is unique in that there is a willing suspension of disbelief that both actors and audience engage in order to create "drama." It's also distinct from other forms of art because of the balanced relationship of its three participants (actor, script, audience).

Alison: How do we build good relationships with those three?

Jason: The things that nurture the actor/script/audience relationship are *truthful behavior, a clear story, dramatic tension* (that is, two actors pursuing different objectives). The things that hinder this relationship are *deception* (trying to preach a particular line in the guise of a story), *unrecognizable behavior, a lack of clarity in story line, unclear or vague acting.*

Alison: Yes. Drama doesn't communicate arbitrarily. Aristotle named character, story, language, ideas, rhythm and spectacle as the basic elements of drama. It's not that these elements happen in a formulaic way or particular order—but that they all occur in all drama.

Lisa: The drama begins the moment we know what the protagonist wants and resolves when the question is answered "Will she get it or not?" If she gets it, we call it comedy. If not, that's tragedy. Then, there's that beautiful animal traditionally called tragi-comedy; a mix of the two.

Jenny: Drama is life put into story form. It mirrors back to us how hilarious, tragic, confusing, unjust, remarkable and rich the human experience is. It provokes us to look at what our lives are about and, at its best, causes us to

grow and change. It is subversive. It has the wonderful ability to slip underneath our defense mechanisms and influence our paradigm on life.

Lisa: A drama is a story. But it isn't the whole story. The word *drama* comes from the Greek word *dran*, which means *to do, to act*. The drama is the *point of action* within a larger story. Drama is distinguished from novel because it does not concern itself with expositing the motivations of its characters, nor in telling the *whole* story. Characters in drama unfold by what they *do*, not by what they *think*. Also, the entire portraits of the characters' lives are not revealed to the audience—only the part of the back story which is crucial for the audience to understand the current action of the story.

Susi: Most of us are most familiar with the drama seen in film and television. The impact on us is huge. It is difficult to measure how significantly stories from these media have affected us. I find myself grappling with the most basic human questions through great drama. I am also entertained. However, the best drama entertains and communicates profound truth. Drama can be comedic or tragic, musical or horrific, and if it rings of truth, it touches our core.

Bruce: The best I've seen are small *slice of life* pieces that show someone given pause, the first inklings of change or consideration. Like much art, the smaller it gets, the more condensed and difficult it becomes to do well. Short stories are an art form in themselves.

Alison: Yes! In Jesus' teachings, in our experience of the gospel, isn't it really in the daily stuff where the real life decisions get made? It's going to the banquet or not, spending our money one way or another, choosing to forgive or get bitter. The meaning of life shows up at the grocery store.

Daniel: I think it's most interesting when we're presented with a world that is true to the struggle we walk in every day.

Jenny: In drama we intentionally create as we condense truths and experiences in life and perform them. But the fact of the matter is, we have condensed and staged drama because life itself is filled with stories.

Jason: But drama creates a *safe* environment to look at life. (*It's just a play.*) At the same time, since drama and stories are so key to shaping our identity it's an extremely powerful medium. Drama raises questions we hadn't thought of. It reflects parts of our behavior we'd prefer not to look at. It stretches our thinking. It does this in a format that relies on the imagination.

Susi: Great stories define our culture, and drama—whether on stage or in film—brings a story into the public arena for scrutiny and shared experience. The stage for the ancient Greeks was a place of worship, where human beings struggled with great life ques-

tions and gods sometimes answered. I believe film has taken over this role in our culture, but stage drama will always hold a unique and powerful place in Christian worship.

Alison: There isn't anything more dramatic than the story of God and his people. It's kind of amazing drama has been so *absent* from worship.

Jenny: Yes, because it's God's story that connects us. Everyone has a story. Everyone has their own drama going on. On top of that God has his mega-drama going amidst all of the little dramas to create the final masterpiece.

Daniel: It's like drama throws complex and contradictory words into one sentence. Drama, at its best, has caused me to ask deep questions about my life and the lives of people around me. I love when I go into a theater and see the gospel in a piece of art that is not explicitly about the gospel.

Alison: But then, so often what isn't explicitly *about* the gospel still deals with gospel issues—because they're human issues. Which is why they're complex and contradictory. And even kind of scary to think about.

Jenny: The bottom line is that drama expressed at its highest potential is prophetic. It is fearless and volatile. It raises issues that people want to ignore. It wants to be the pebble in your shoe that you can't pretend to not notice. It aims to provoke and disturb. It can serve as an alarm clock to people whose souls feel too sleepy to care about certain issues or truths in life. From the stage it sounds off: *Wake up!*

Daniel: And it works because it allows the audience to sit in the tension. If drama remains open-ended, which I prefer, it doesn't force-feed you hope on a spoonful of sugar, but it allows you to *find* hope or despair. It's your choice. What will your world look like? It is never the drama's job to determine your world for you.

Nina: Right. The actors don't spell it out for us, telling us what we should think or feel—they think and feel and *show us*. We laugh with and cry with the actors on stage because they have touched on the truth—how things are, or how we so much wish they were.

Scott: One of the things I like about drama (and I suppose this might be true for all art) is that it's indirect. It doesn't have to be—and perhaps can't be—autobiographical. There is little appeal, for artist or audience, to watching someone talk directly about who they are or what they feel: Imagine me handing out little 3x5 cards describing my soul as I currently perceive it! But if I can take a small, true piece of my soul, in its darkness and light, and draw it out through the dialogue and actions of people on a stage, then something deep and appealing is going on.

Jenny: And then drama is redemptive. The writer, director and actors take situations and relationships from everyday life, learn from them and discover truth about human nature. They craft their learning into art and offer it to the audience. The hope is that what has been learned from life is communicated through the drama, not as lecture but as experience—indirectly. Good art does not stay on the stage but walks out the door when the play is over. In a way, the audience *is* the drama's work of living, breathing art. This art can continue in the people that it affects.

Daniel: It raises questions and represents current and contextual struggle. It offers an opportunity to respond. It engages a community by gathering people together in a live setting where the audience has to interact with live people telling a story. Drama shows us where we've been and offers possibilities as to where we might be headed.

Jenny: Drama also reveals the redemptive side of the painful realities of life. It takes brutal parts of history and, without skewing the truth, transforms them into something beautiful and full of meaning. It has the power to reveal goodness that is usually overshadowed by pain as well as the power to lead an audience into recognizing that goodness.

PART 2
What Isn't Drama?

Jason: What isn't drama? Propaganda. Attempts to emotionally manipulate an audience. Lectures.

Bruce: So much of the "Christian drama" I have seen is dull: propaganda in story form. The story is only the message bearer.

Daniel: Drama is not art when it belittles reality and ties things up in neat little packages. It shouldn't preach or attempt to manipulate.

Jason: Yes. Drama shouldn't try to preach a sermon. One of the things that drama does well is bring up the complexity of life . . . so it shouldn't be used to try to oversimplify situations.

Lisa: When a drama is preachy, it weighs the action of the play down and prevents the most beautiful moments from surfacing. I saw a Christian production once that was hard to watch. In theater we get to know and care for the character through what she does to get over her obstacles to what she wants. *This* character preached at and tried to convert his non-Christian friend through the whole play. He flawlessly endured persecution, then judged others who weren't as strong as he. So, what did we learn about the character? He's preachy, self-righteous and comes off pretty arrogant . . . he wasn't likeable.

Daniel: I watched a sketch at a conference about dealing with conflict. Aside from the fact that it was waaay cheezy, it also tried to be a sermon. We got to watch the man hide something from his friends, then have it exposed, then have a fight about it, then have everyone say, "That's okay, we still love you" in the end. It was sort of like "The Five Steps to Conflict Resolution" in skit form. And, of course, nobody is going to walk out of that room and have conflict the way the sketch presented it.

Scott: Drama fails when it becomes a "tool"—when there's nothing of the artist's or audience's souls involved.

Nina: Yes, drama wants to say something—but it's the saying it that matters, not the focus on a specific outcome in the audience (e.g., everyone signing up).

Scott: I hate drama that I think is trying to influence me toward some preplanned action: "Watch this dialogue. Now invite Jesus into your heart." As though I can't be trusted enough to be truly emotionally engaged by what I see and therefore need a sort of prepackaged set of emotional responses.

Nina: That seems more mercenary and manipulative to me than I believe drama is or should be.

Alison: It uses the audience.

Jason: To leave the audience out of the relationship so that an actor can vent a lot of emotion may feel good for the actor, but it's abusing drama.

Daniel: It is one thing for the author of a play or sketch to demonstrate what he or she would do, but if the sketch preaches, then the audience isn't left with anything to discuss. When the audience is shown how to respond, they are cut off from taking ownership. We need to let the drama seep in and swirl around them, and then they can respond.

Nina: There are commercials I would consider drama—"This is your brain on drugs . . . and this is your family, relationships . . ."—but most are just commercials designed to get us to buy stuff, even the Kodak commercials. What's the difference? The first is sort of a performance art picture of how things really are. The second are moments choreographed to get a specific audience response rather than to tell a true story. I still cry during Kodak commercials, but I know I'm being manipulated. The fact that we joke about it (Kodak moment, anyone?) means we know exactly what the writers were after.

Scott: If the writers were trying to get something from us, then it's bad drama. Bad drama denies the mystery of God and our souls; good drama invites us into that mystery.

Susi: Drama isn't spectacle. Public gags, extravagant art and special effects on stage do not constitute drama. Story is essential to drama. Drama isn't private. Drama takes private thoughts and feelings and puts them on the public stage. Drama is a form of proclamation.

Alison: Sometimes it seems like drama isn't bad but, rather, badly used. And sometimes both. It's critical that we know what we are hoping the drama will do in the context. Is it telling a story, straight up? Is it pointing at something prophetically? Is it making Scripture accessible? That affects what and how we write.

Nina: There are also just plain badly written sketches and shows—superficial, going for the easy connection or communicating what could easily be said in a sentence: "Jesus died for my sins," or, "Life is meaningless." These are deep concepts but often communicated quite superficially in our churches and even onstage. Most people aren't gripped or provoked by that sort of drama.

Bruce: Are you sketching out a quick cartoon for a family joke? Then much is forgiven and more is not needed. Are you trying to get a stranger's heart with an art form? Don't embarrass yourself with quick and shoddy work, and don't be gulled by the compliments of friends.

Jason: Exactly. Often, well-meaning Christians ill-conceive drama.

They desire to illustrate biblical truth and use a combination of different theatrical techniques (most often a combination of allegory and melodrama) to try to illustrate a point or emotionally stir an audience. As an audience member, I am left guessing, *Am I watching an allegory (a very complicated thing to do well theatrically) or a melodrama? Is this behavior symbolic? Is it supposed to be real? Who are these characters? Why are they wearing signs? Is this hokey? Am I supposed to laugh? Cry?*

Alison: I've heard plenty of talky stuff, where the sketch is supposed to explain the entirety of the gospel or missions or a person's life. But life is just not like that. None of us talks our way through—we *do*. We act. Bad drama is often bad because it says too much.

Susi: Although the words *are* important. I enjoy going to the Museum of Modern Art and looking at static art pieces, but if I go to see a drama, I expect words. That doesn't mean it must be lots of words. It does mean that the drama onstage hangs together by a story.

Lisa: If I'm writing a play, it's not meant to be read. It's meant to be seen and experienced.

Alison: So our hope for drama is to have it taken in through the experience rather than just the hearing. But both what we see and what we hear is crucial. That has application for every aspect of communicating the gospel to postmoderns, doesn't it?

Susi: Actually, the traditional Mass comes close to postmodern hearts, with the experience of taking the Eucharist as the climax of the worship service. I believe drama also can be this climax. Good drama can take the sermon to a higher plane. This is not to say that the sermon isn't important. It is to say that the Word becoming flesh before the eyes of the audience will have more impact than three points of application.

Alison: So the key is *experiencing* the hearing rather than simply hearing *from* the drama. Words are important—but it's much more than words. Words have a job to do.

Lisa: The minute characters launch into long speeches explaining the past and how they got to this current place, they stop the action of the play. Action moves drama. Exposition stops it. When I say "action," I don't mean action as we see it in action movies. I mean what the characters do to get what they want. So, you only want to include necessary exposition. Sketches that try to preach say too much and miss the movement of the story.

Jason: Once I saw a play that was "semi-autobiographical" put together for an outreach. In this particular case, the woman who wrote the play was also starring in it as the main character. Two-thirds of the way into the play the woman was crying and screaming and ranting about how bad her life was. At the point that the woman was the most emotionally intense, much of the audience left. Or sat awkwardly waiting for this part to be done. Why? Because she was abusing drama. The drama seemed to serve her need to vent a lot of emotion, but it didn't invite the audience into discovering some truth.

Daniel: It's kind of like Jesus telling parables. Jesus doesn't just lay it out there for all the world to see. He keeps things hidden so that they can be found. So that people take ownership by seeking and finding. That is the response we should be hoping for.

Alison: It's not dramatic to spill all the info right from the start. People stay in their seats because they expect something still to come. Yakking everything from the stage from the beginning leaves the audience no reason to keep listening. And it overexplains realities that can't be explained—and, in fact, are misrepresented by explanation.

Daniel: You often have a character in the play that functions as the mouthpiece for the playwright. But that only works when it is not forced on the audience. It's usually pretty clear, in most good drama, where the author stands, but then the author trusts his or her audience to come to some of their own conclusions.

Alison: Perhaps our problem is that it's hard to let go and allow people to draw their own conclusions. Maybe in the church we've exerted ourselves to-

ward controlling things—so we can have orthodoxy with the outcome we want and the gospel preached just so. I mean, not that we'd want it preached sloppily—but maybe we've thought God to be less able than he is to ensure the right outcome of communication. I mean, people's hearts are God's, not ours, to shape. Our job is to tell the truth the best we can.

Scott: I've seen a good bit of drama that I think would be better classified as propaganda shows—sort of a Christianized version of why we are all happy on the collective farm. It strikes me as a somewhat ironic attempt at maintaining some of those controls.

Jason: Seeing bad Christian drama and hearing suspicion of non-Christian theater from other believers caused some serious problems for me. I felt like in order to do good art, I needed to be outside the church, but in order to be connected at church, I needed to stay away from the theater. The false dichotomy between good theater and the church caused me to resent both communities and feel out of sorts. When drama is abused or ill-conceived, I get frustrated and angry. Others I know have become suspicious of using drama in church.

Daniel: Yes. And when bad art gets produced, it strengthens people's assumptions that all art done by Christians will be bad. I've experienced the difficulty of walking into a performance and having it assumed that it is going to be bad because I am Christian and what I am performing has the label of Christian theater slapped on it. Christians have the best story to tell, but we haven't yet learned how to tell it well.